If you were a

QUART *or a* LITER

by Marcie Aboff

illustrated by Francesca Carabelli

PICTURE WINDOW BOOKS
Minneapolis, Minnesota

MILK

JUICE

WATER

Editors: Christianne Jones and Jill Kalz
Designer: Lori Bye
Page Production: Melissa Kes
Art Director: Nathan Gassman
Editorial Director: Nick Healy
The illustrations in this book were created with acrylics.

Picture Window Books
151 Good Counsel Drive
P.O. Box 669
Mankato, MN 56002-0669
877-845-8392
www.picturewindowbooks.com

Printed in the United States of America.

 All books published by Picture Window Books
are manufactured with paper containing at least
10 percent post-consumer waste.

Library of Congress Cataloging-in-Publication Data
Aboff, Marcie.
If you were a quart or a liter / by Marcie Aboff ; illustrated by
Francesca Carabelli.
p. cm. — (Math Fun)
Includes index.
ISBN 978-1-4048-5207-5 (library binding)
ISBN 978-1-4048-5208-2 (paperback)
1. Quart (Unit)—Juvenile literature. 2. Liter—Juvenile literature.
3. Units of measurement—Juvenile literature. I. Carabelli,
Francesca, ill. II. Title.
QC104.A26 2009
530.8'1—dc22   2008037912

Special thanks to our adviser for his expertise:

Stuart Farm, M.Ed., Mathematics Lecturer
University of North Dakota

quart—a unit of English capacity measurement
liter—a unit of metric capacity measurement

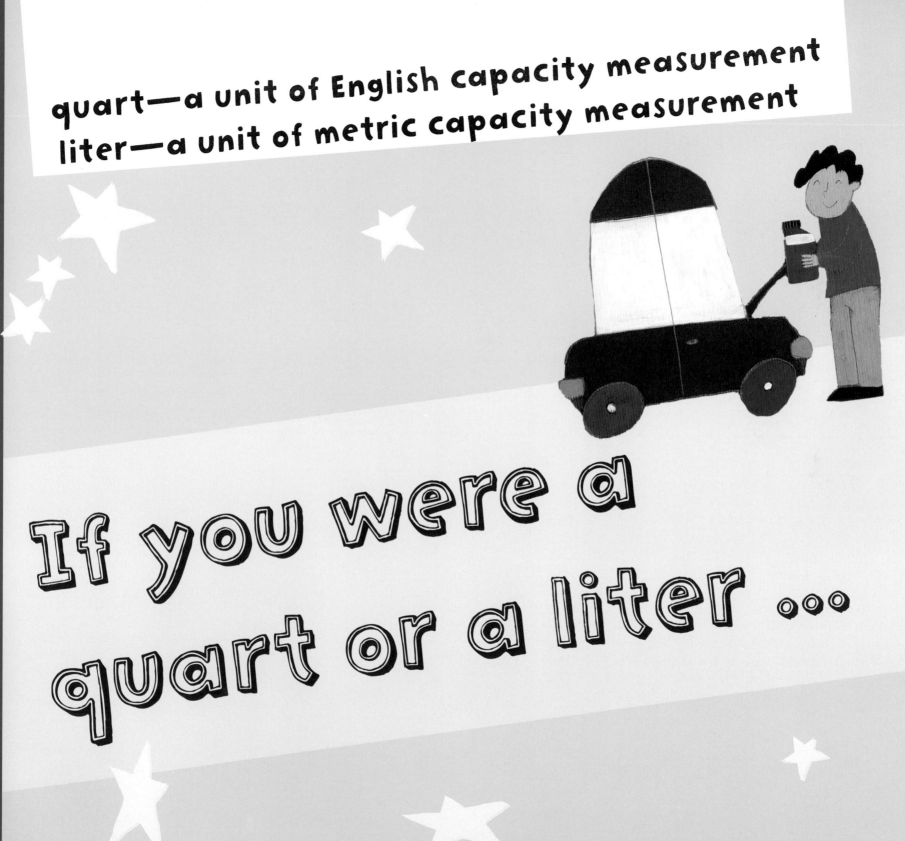

If you were a quart or a liter ...

... you could be containers of milk, juice, and water. You would be found all over the supermarket!

MILK

JUICE

WATER

If you were a quart, you would measure the amount that a container can hold. There would be four of you in 1 gallon.

Cody made 1 quart of chocolate ice cream.
Carly made 1 quart of rocky road.
Claire made 2 quarts of strawberry shortcake.

4 quarts = 1 gallon

The calves mixed their ice cream together and made 1 gallon of a new flavor.

If you were a liter, you would also measure the amount that a container can hold. One liter is just a little bigger than 1 quart.

It's the hottest day of the year.
To cool down, Lucy drinks 1 liter of lemonade.
Ira drinks 1 quart of iced tea.

That hits the spot!

If you were a quart, you would always have 2 pints or 4 cups in you.

Rory and Roxy raced outside during recess. Rory opened his quart-sized bottle of water.

Rory drank half, and Roxy drank half.
They each drank 1 pint, or 2 cups, of water.

1 cup
1 cup
1 pint

1 cup
1 pint
1 cup

1 quart = 2 pints or 4 cups

If you were a liter, you would have 1,000 milliliters in you.

Penny is serving punch at her party.

She pours 1,000 milliliters (1 liter) of soda and 2,000 milliliters (2 liters) of fruit juice into a bowl. That's 3,000 milliliters, or 3 liters, of punch.

If you were a quart or a liter, you could be changed into one another. In fact, 1 quart is about 0.95 liters, and 1 liter is about 1.1 quarts.

Pip needs 1 quart of cranberry juice and 5 quarts of orange juice. Mr. Nye sells juice by the liter only.

1 quart = about 0.95 liters
1 liter = about 1.1 quarts

Pip says, "I'd like about 1 liter of cranberry juice and about 4 and three-fourths liters of orange juice, please."

If you were a quart or a liter, you could be shortened. The words *quart* and *quarts* can be replaced with the letters *qt*. The words *liter* and *liters* can be replaced with the letter *L*.

Hannah won lots of new cooking supplies in a cooking contest. Her new blender held 2 liters.

The mini chopper held 1 quart, and the slow cooker held 6 quarts.

1qt

6qt

FIRST PLACE HANNAH

1

If you were a quart, you could be a bottle of motor oil.

Joe put 1 quart of oil in his small car.

Bob put 3 quarts of oil in his medium-sized car.

Jim put 4 quarts of oil in his large truck.
Together, they put in 8 quarts, or 2 gallons, of oil.

If you were a liter, you could be a plastic soda bottle.

Holly stocked up on soda for the summer picnic. She bought 5 2-liter bottles of grape and 10 2-liter bottles of orange.

That's 30 liters of soda!

You would be a real thirst quencher ...
... if you were a quart or a liter.

HOW MUCH DOES IT HOLD?

Gather a collection of different mugs, glasses, and other containers. Fill each with water. With a friend, take turns guessing how much water each container holds. Guess in both quarts (or cups or pints) and liters. Check the answers by pouring the water into a large measuring cup.

Glossary

capacity—the total amount a container can hold

cup—a unit of English capacity measurement;
   there are 4 cups in 1 quart

gallon—a unit of English capacity measurement;
   there are 4 quarts in 1 gallon

liter—a unit of metric capacity measurement
   (1 liter = 1.1 quarts)

milliliter—a unit of metric capacity measurement;
   there are 1,000 milliliters in 1 liter

pint—a unit of English capacity measurement;
   there are 2 pints in 1 quart

quart—a unit of English capacity
   measurement (1 quart = 0.95 liters)

To Learn More

More Books to Read

deRubertis, Barbara. *Lulu's Lemonade.* New York:
   Kane Press, 2000.

Trumbauer, Lisa. *What Is Volume?* New York:
   Children's Press, 2006.

On the Web

FactHound offers a safe, fun way to find educator-approved
Internet sites related to this book.

Here's what you do:

   1. Visit **www.facthound.com**

   2. Choose your grade level.

   3. Begin your search.

This book's ID number is 9781404852075

Index

Look for all of the books in the Math Fun series:

If You Were a Divided-by Sign

If You Were a Fraction

If You Were a Minus Sign

If You Were a Minute

If You Were a Plus Sign

If You Were a Pound or a Kilogram

If You Were a Quart or a Liter

If You Were a Set

If You Were a Times Sign

If You Were an Even Number

If You Were an Inch or a Centimeter

If You Were an Odd Number